Good Grief,

Great Grace

Finding Light After Darkness: A Journey Through Unimaginable Loss

by

Roschelle Ogbuji

ISBN: 979-8-218-53623-7

West-Woods Publishing, LLC

395 Sawdust Rd, Suite 2049

The Woodlands, TX 77380

www.WestWoodsPublishing.com

Cover and book design by Roschelle Ogbuji

Book layout by Roschelle Ogbuji

Photography courtesy of Roschelle Ogbuji and Monique West-Fielder

TABLE OF CONTENTS

PREFACE

Writing has always been my refuge, a way to express emotions that I could not easily share. Ever since I was a little girl, I loved writing. I kept journals—so many journals—since the third grade, capturing my thoughts, my dreams, and my struggles. Writing gave me a voice, and in those pages, I found solace and healing. I kept journals for every part of my life—personal reflections, spiritual notes, even the joys and challenges of love. It was a way to give shape to my feelings, to release what was locked inside.

When I was in college, I took creative writing classes and discovered a love for poetry. I could sit for hours, letting the words flow effortlessly. It was cathartic, and it came naturally to me. Writing always allowed me to process my experiences and find meaning, and it helped me heal.

But when I lost my three daughters, everything changed. People would ask, "When are you going to write a book?"

And every time I tried, I found I couldn't. The words that had always come so easily were suddenly out of reach. The grief was overwhelming, and it held my voice hostage. I knew deep down that I needed to heal before I could even begin to write this story. The pain was too raw, too real, and I avoided revisiting those memories because I feared being consumed by them.

What I found, though, was that I could talk about it. Speaking came more easily than writing. I could share my story out loud, even when putting pen to paper felt impossible. This book began with those spoken words—words that eventually found their way onto the page, capturing moments from my life that forever changed me.

Revisiting that time, reliving those emotions, was frightening. I had to be honest with myself: I couldn't do it alone. The first time I faced this pain, I had God, but I lacked someone physically present to help hold that space with me. I needed someone to walk this journey by my side, someone who could help me navigate the darkness and give me the courage to face those memories again. Thankfully, the universe provided that person—a partner who walked this path with me, held my hand, and helped me turn my spoken story into written words.

This book is for anyone who has experienced loss. It is for those who have felt alone in their grief, for those who are searching for healing. Nothing can erase the pain of losing my girls, but sharing this story has allowed me to find some measure of peace. I hope that by reading these words, you too will find strength, healing, and the glimmer of hope that even in the midst of unimaginable loss, grace can be found.

We are never truly alone. I invite you to join me on this journey—to find hope, to find healing, and to know that even when life brings us to our knees, we can still rise.

With love and grace,

Roschelle Ogbuji

CHAPTER 1: THE FOUNDATION OF FAITH AND FAMILY

I can still vividly remember the love that surrounded me in my childhood. My earliest memories are filled with the immense love my parents had for me, and I was certain of it in everything they did. After working long hours at Ford Motor Company, they would find time to take us on bike rides, walks in the park, the bookstore, skating and annual family vacations. My parents were both Christians, but they had two different faith expressions. My mother a Pentecostal and Charismatic and my father who was an American Baptist. Humorously I refer to myself as "Bapticostal" because I have a firm understanding of theological concepts but drenched in the power of the Holy Spirit.

I focused more on the heart of God and the work and the power of the Holy Spirit. So, growing up I had a balanced understanding that God was not just something I need to think about, but something that I had to also experience with my heart. I found myself leaning more of the experiential notion of God because that is where I felt that connection the most.

My father who was a part-time minister used to practice his sermons in front of me, not just simple scripture recitations, but complex, theological conversations. I was only in second or third grade, but my father would engage me in discussions about the rapture, grace, and the different promises God made throughout scripture. These weren't just bedtime stories; they were lessons in faith, responsibility, and a deeper understanding of God's purpose.

I've always been a good listener, equally as much as I am a communicator. I remember sitting with my dad, listening intently, absorbing every word. My inquisitive nature meant I had plenty of questions, and both my father and mother encouraged that curiosity. From a young age, I had a deep sense of something greater than myself—something spiritual. Even as a child, I knew that I was connected to something beyond the physical world.

I spent a lot of time with my great-grandmother, Sadie Hollowell, who had a rich and complicated life. She was a Cherokee, Choctaw, and Ghanaian woman who lived through extraordinary times. At one point in her life, she was a bootlegger and a madam, but when she found God, she co-founded one of the largest Black megachurches in Kansas City. Spending time with her wasn't just about family; it was about absorbing the history, the lessons, and the strength that came from a woman who had lived through so much. My great-grandmother was also instrumental in the early days of Liberty University, which I later attended to get my master's degree. It felt like a full circle moment.

Her faith, though, was unlike anything I had ever seen. I remember her breaking into gospel songs while hanging clothes on the line, tears streaming down her face as she praised God. I was just six or seven years old, but even then, I knew I wanted to have faith like that someday. She had lived through such unimaginable hardships—her father was one of the last slaves brought from Ghana—and yet, her faith remained unshakable. Her tears were not tears of sorrow; they were tears of praise. Watching her worship God so fully and openly left a lasting impact on me.

Another pivotal figure in my life was my grandmother. She didn't have much, but she was proud and self- sufficient, refusing help from anyone. I spent hours with her, soaking in her stories. She would tell me about her life growing up, the struggles she faced, and how at one point, she even passed for white. She had red hair and green eyes, and she looked more like a white woman than a Black woman, something that gave her a unique perspective on race relations in America. I remember her distrust of white people, stemming from her experiences of what was said about Black people when she was in the room, but no one knew her true identity. Her stories were raw, real, and filled with both pain and resilience.

One of the most defining moments of my childhood came after my grandmother passed. My family was searching for her insurance papers, and they couldn't find them. That night, my grandmother came to me in a dream and told me exactly where they were. When I told my mother, she was in disbelief, but sure enough, they were exactly where my grandmother said they would be. This experience confirmed for me that I had a spiritual gift, but it scared me. My dreams were too real, too vivid. I would have recurring dreams of my grandmother, and it frightened me so much that I prayed for God to mute my gift until I was ready to use it.

Despite my spiritual awareness, I was self-conscious growing up. I wasn't outgoing, but I was friendly and funny. In retrospect, I can see that I was also a bit obnoxious, often seeking validation from others because I didn't like myself very much. But deep down, I knew I was a kind person. My parents worked hard to provide a middle-class life for us, and they instilled in us the values of kindness, love, and a strong work ethic. But above all else, they taught me to put God first.

I was raised to understand that life is about more than just surviving; it's about seeking God in everything. "Seek ye first the kingdom of God, and all these things will be added unto you" was a scripture that shaped my life. My parents made sacrifices to ensure that we had access to education and experiences they didn't have growing up. My father, in particular, gave me the freedom to explore my faith, which led to a significant turning point in my life.

When I was about 13, I went through a phase where I questioned everything, including my faith. I remember telling my dad that I didn't think I was a Christian anymore, that I felt indoctrinated and wanted to find my own path. Rather than being angry, my dad told me that while I didn't have to go to his church, I had to go somewhere. That began my journey of exploring different ideologies, both within and outside of Christianity. Eventually, I found my way back to the church through music, starting a gospel choir at DePaul University in Chicago.

Looking back now, I see that my upbringing, my experiences, and the stories passed down from my ancestors were the foundation of who I am today. They shaped my faith, my resilience, and my understanding of the world. The black church, especially, was not just a place of worship; it was a place of politics, community, and culture. It gave me the tools to navigate a predominantly white world while staying grounded in my identity as a Black woman.

Before the tragedy, my dreams were simple: I wanted to be a good mother, to raise my children, and to one day be a grandmother. I had a career in marketing and public relations, and I was pursuing the American dream. But after the fire, everything changed. Those dreams didn't disappear, but they took on a new meaning. Today, I still hold on to the lessons my parents and ancestors taught me: to seek God in all things, to love fully, and to live with purpose. That day would change everything. What started as a routine day in the life of our family would soon be marked by a tragedy no one could have predicted. The fire came without warning, turning our world upside down.

CHAPTER 2: THE FIRE

November 30th, 2007 is a date etched into my mind forever. It started as a normal day, taking my then husband Chukwuma's family shopping while they were visiting from England. I remember spending the day watching Chika, Anya and Imose trying on dresses. I remember having a wonderful experience with them, meeting their relatives for the first time. We took lots of photos and even went to the park earlier that day. We then grabbed some pizza for dinner for the girls. When I put the girls down for the night, I remember the Wizard of Oz was playing on TV, so I kept it playing so they could watch it from their cribs. Later, Chukwuma's cousins wanted to see a movie later that evening, so we went to watch American Gangster. To this day, I can't sit in a movie theater without my children because of what happened that night. After the movie, we grabbed dinner at the Winking Lizard, and I checked in with the two babysitters (then ages 12 and 14) that I called earlier to see if they could stay a little longer. Everything seemed fine. We even stopped for gas on the way home, and as we drove, I heard sirens in the distance. I didn't think much of it until we turned onto our block.

As we approached, my heart stopped. The entire street was blocked off with fire trucks, EMS vehicles, and police cars. Something inside me screamed that something was wrong. I called the house, but the phone went straight to voicemail. That's when the panic set in. My thoughts spiraled: Were the girls, okay? What happened? Why is the street blocked off? As we made it to the other end of the street, I noticed all the commotion was centered around our house. We got out of the car, and I saw smoke billowing out of our house. My heart dropped to the pit of my stomach. I kept asking where the girls were, but no one could meet my eyes. I was met with silence.

Once we told the police we were the homeowners, we were quickly escorted to a neighbor's house, where several first-responders were stationed. Over five times I asked, "Where are my girls?" But I was only met with blank stares. That's when a police officer approached us. He told me they were taking us to the hospital where the girls were. I was praying, hoping, desperately clinging to the idea that everything would be okay. Please let them be okay. I tried calling Vincent who was Imose's father and my first husband, but I couldn't get through. Imose was supposed to be at his house that night, but she wanted to stay to hang out with the baby-sitters. That decision has haunted me ever since—what if she hadn't been there? What if...

When we arrived at the hospital, the emergency room lobby was empty. I felt like I was in a fog. Seconds felt like a lifetime, waiting for someone to tell me where my girls were. When the doctor came out, the words he said didn't make sense: Two of your daughters have passed away. Your third daughter is fighting for her life. My mind couldn't comprehend what he was saying. How? Why? What are you talking about? I thought, just a few hours ago, they were alive. How could they be gone now? It felt like my world had stopped. It felt like I was hit in face with a 2x4. Everything in my brain shut down, like someone had pulled the plug. That moment, I know, is when my life changed forever. I felt this overwhelming surge of anger building inside me, like fire in my gut. My mind was racing. There were many questions. What Happened?

Where were the babysitters? How are my girls dead. But then I heard a quiet voice within my spirit say: Don't let anger consume you. And just like that, I felt my anxiety subside, a sense of stillness that only God could have given me. I then began to make calls to my mother and father.

Vincent and my father-in-law went back to the hospital room to identify the girls, but I knew better. I knew I couldn't do it. I heard that same voice telling me: Don't go back there, you don't want that image in your mind forever. Sometime later, they both told me how much they regretted seeing what they did. It confirmed what I already knew—I wasn't supposed to see that.

The hospital staff then told me they needed to life-flight Anya to Akron Children's Hospital. They said she had a better chance of survival there because they had iron lungs. I couldn't even process what was happening. My mind was still racing. How was I going to live without my two babies? My father-in-law drove us to Akron, and during that drive, I remember pleading with God: Please, God, let Anya live. I don't want to be here without my girls. I don't know how to live without them. And then, in that moment, I heard that same voice: No devastation will ever outshine My glory and Anya will live on. I didn't understand it at the time, but those words gave me something to hold on to, which was hope.

When we arrived in Akron, I was met with another harsh reality. Seeing Anya laying there holding on by a thread, but her chances were slim. I was torn between grief for Imose and Chika and desperation for Anya to survive. I felt a dichotomy of emotions. I was grateful to have Anya, but every time I thought about Imose and Chika, I would burst into tears. The doctors said they were doing everything they could, but deep down, I knew I had to prepare myself for the worst.

It was later, in the days after the fire, that I found out more of what had happened. The fire had started in the family room on the first floor. The two babysitters woke up to find the room engulfed in flames. Imose who had been sleeping on the sofa with the babysitters was sent to the front door, while they rushed upstairs to get Chika and Anya. But then, something called a flashover happened—all the oxygen in the room was sucked out, and everything combusted. Imose didn't make it to the door. She was caught in the flash and died instantly. The babysitters, in their panic, tried to devise a plan in which one of them would jump out of a window and the other one would lower the babies down. When the oldest babysitter jumped out, she shattered her ankle and left the younger babysitter on the second floor with the girls. The oxygen level was depleting, and she saw the fire trucks coming. She also jumped out of the window, breaking her leg. When the firefighters arrived, the babysitters were in shock due to their injuries. The firefighters didn't know there were additional children were still in the house until one of my neighbors shouted, "There are babies inside!".

While at the hospital as Anya fought for her life, I also learned that our homeowner's insurance had lapsed, which was another blow. Letters had been coming in the mail, but between taking care of three children, working, and dealing with everything else, I hadn't opened them. Now, not only had I lost my girls, but we had no insurance to cover the damage. But I was so beyond broken at that point that even this seemed insignificant in comparison to losing my children.

The next few days were a blur. My family and friends started arriving from all over the country. The community rallied around us. People showed up at the hospital for prayer vigils for Anya and well-wishes. My dear friend Andrea organized everything including managing donations for clothes, food and gift cards. It was overwhelming to see how many people were impacted by our loss. The fire didn't just happen to me; it happened to our entire community. The grief was shared by so many.

I think back to that night often. There are no words to describe the depth of the pain, the anger, and the disbelief I felt. English doesn't even have a term for parents who lose children. When you are a child that loses a parent you are called an orphan. When are a spouse that loses their spouse, you are a widow. But those of us that lose children, we are the consider "the unspoken". Because it is every parent's worst fear, we don't speak about losing children. For those of us that have, there are no words that can describe this feeling. But in the midst of what was not spoken, God was there, carrying me through. And while I will never fully understand why this happened, I knew that God was the only way to see myself through. In the aftermath of the fire, we had to face the incomprehensible task of saying goodbye. The funeral was the first step in that long journey of grief, but nothing could have prepared me for the overwhelming emotions that came with laying my daughters to rest.

CHAPTER 3: THE FUNERAL

The funeral for my daughters was unlike anything I had ever imagined, a moment that would become both a final goodbye and a celebration of their short, beautiful lives. While we were at the hospital with Anya, my dear friend Andrea had taken the reins, bringing everyone together to start planning the funeral for Imose and Chika. She kept telling me, "Your church won't hold all the people who want to come." I couldn't quite grasp it at the time, but she was right. The overwhelming support from the community was beyond what I could have anticipated.

We ultimately chose First Baptist on Fairmount in Shaker Heights, a church that could hold 1,500 people. And to my shock, every seat was filled. It was a sea of people, all gathered to honor my girls, and I remember feeling both humbled and terrified at the same time.

My mother-in-law didn't want me to speak at the funeral. She thought that if I cried, it would be embarrassing. But I knew I was supposed to cry—I was burying my daughters, after all. Anyone who would judge me for that was missing the point entirely. This was the last time I could ever speak about my girls in such a public way. I didn't get to plan their graduations, their weddings, or be there when they walked down the aisle. So, this funeral was my only chance to honor them in the way I loved them.

Picking out the casket was one of the hardest things I've ever had to do. We decided to cremate Chika, but Vincent and I did not want to put Imose through the fire again. We needed special permission from the county to bury multiple bodies in one grave, but we got it. When Andrea asked me what kind of casket I wanted, I just said, "Something pink." The same answer I gave when asked what color dress I wanted for Imose. Pink was their favorite color, and that's all I could focus on.

My gospel choir from college came to support me. Friends flew in from all over the country, and my heart was so full knowing they were by my side. I'll never forget the overwhelming love in that room. I didn't have to do this alone; my family, friends and community were all there helping me carry this unbearable weight.

I was terrified to go to the funeral. Absolutely terrified. I kept thinking, this would be the last time I would see them. The funeral wasn't an open casket, but the funeral home asked if I wanted to see Imose before she was buried. I heard a voice inside me say yet again, "Don't go back there. You don't want that memory." And I was obedient. The last time I saw Imose was when I said goodbye to her that evening before the fire. I wanted that to be the last memory I carried with me.

We buried my daughters at Cleveland Memorial Gardens on Green Road. It's a beautiful, modern cemetery, and that was important to me. I didn't want an old, overgrown cemetery. I wanted something that looked fresh, where new life could continue to grow. The thought of my daughters in an old cemetery unsettled me. But when it came to the gravestone, I couldn't do it. I couldn't bring myself to put their names on a gravestone. To this day, I haven't. I still wonder if I'll ever be ready.

My mother-in-law insisted that we all wear black. I didn't

want that. I wanted something bright, something that represented life, not death. Afterall, these were little girls in the prime of their childhood. I wanted to wear pink, with butterflies—symbols of transformation. But I wasn't strong enough to fight her on it, so we wore black. I still regret that I didn't stand my ground.

At the funeral, I had asked my pastor not to preach a sermon of sorrow. I wanted something filled with hope, something that invited people to know who God is. The choir sang four songs, and they sang I Can Only Imagine by Mercy Me, which had been Imose's favorite. I vividly remember standing up during that song, tears streaming down my face, and praising God. I don't know where I found the strength. I wasn't inconsolable; I was grateful. Grateful that God hadn't left me, even though I was so angry with Him. I kept hearing a voice, "Hold on to God. You will need Him to get through this."

When it came time for me to speak, I didn't write anything down. I knew whatever I said would come from my heart. My heart was racing as I struggled to walk up to the pulpit. I spoke about my daughters and the immense joy they brought into my life. I even made people laugh, sharing stories about their little antics. I remember telling the joke about Anya arriving in heaven three days late, and the whole room cracked up. In that moment, I felt the weight lift off me, if only for a little while.

As the choir sang, I looked at the stained-glass window behind them, and the sun came pouring through. It was like something out of a movie. For me, on that December 7th day, it was my small miracle. It was a glimmer of hope in the bleakest moment of my life, a reminder that God was still with me.

The repass after the funeral was a bittersweet moment. I was surrounded by love—my family, my choirs, my friends and community—but there was still a profound sadness that we had come together under such tragic circumstances. Some of them had never even met Chika or Anya, and that broke my heart.

Through it all, I just kept asking God to give me the strength to get through this in my right mind. I didn't want to lose myself wholly in grief. I didn't want to give up on life. I wanted to honor my girls by continuing to live, by holding on to hope, by clinging to God even when I didn't understand His plan. Leaving the funeral, my thoughts returned to each of my daughters—their personalities, their laughter, and the unique gifts they brought into my life. Imose, my firstborn, was always the leader, a "beautiful gift from God" who touched my heart in ways that will never fade. Her memory would become the first I would carry with me as I embarked on this journey of healing.

CHAPTER 4: IMOSE, MY BEAUTIFUL GIFT FROM GOD

Imose Esosa. Her name means "beautiful gift from God," and that's exactly what she was—a beautiful gift that transformed my life in ways I could never have imagined. I still remember the day I found out I was pregnant with her. I was in Flushing, New York, working as a software trainer.  The city's vibrant streets were filled with the smells of various Asian cuisines, which, to my surprise, suddenly became unbearable to me. That was my first clue. A quick call to my mom confirmed my suspicion—she suggested I might be pregnant. With all the writing in kanji, finding a drugstore felt like navigating a maze, but I managed. And there it was, clear as day—I was going to be a mother.

Imose was not just any child; she was prayed for, longed for. Vincent and I had been asking the Lord to bless us with a child since Christmas, and when January came, our prayers were answered. From the moment I knew she was on her way, everything changed. I started eating better, taking care of myself, and preparing to be the best mother I could be. But more than that, Imose's impending arrival began a deep transformation within me.

During my pregnancy, I found myself confronting long-buried traumas. The thought of bringing a daughter into the world terrified me—not because I feared motherhood, but because I was afraid I wouldn't be enough for her. The scars from my past, particularly the trauma of being molested as a child by my uncle, resurfaced with a vengeance. I realized I needed to heal, not just for myself, but for my daughter. I couldn't let my unresolved pain shape her life.

Therapy became a lifeline during those months. I wanted to ensure that I was emotionally healthy enough to raise a daughter who would know her worth, who would never feel the shame and ugliness that had plagued me for so long. For much of my life, I had believed I was ugly, both inside and out. The mirror reflected a distorted image—a monster that didn't match the beauty I saw in others, especially in my own mother, who I thought was gorgeous. I now know that this was called body dysmorphia, but back then, it was just my reality. I always considered myself the smart and funny girl, never the pretty one.

Naming my daughter was no small task. I believed, and still believe, that names hold power. Each time you say your child's name, you're speaking that identity into them. That's why I chose the name Imose Esosa—"beautiful gift from God." Every time I called her, I was affirming her beauty, her value and her divinity.

When the time came for her to enter the world, the process was anything but easy. I suffered from preeclampsia, a dangerous condition that required me to be induced early. My labor was long and painful, complicated by the events of September 11, 2001—the day before I was scheduled to give birth. The tension of that day, combined with my fears, made my labor even more difficult. My body refused to relax, my mind fixated on the fact that my mother might not be able to reach me because of the attacks. But when she finally arrived, everything changed. With her by my side, I was able to let go, and soon after, my beautiful Imose was born.

The moment I saw her, all my fears and doubts melted away. She was perfect—more beautiful than I could have ever imagined. People always say that love at first sight isn't real, but I knew it was the moment I held her in my arms. I couldn't believe that something so beautiful could come from me. For the next five years, I thanked God every day for the gift of my daughter. She was proof that God was real, that He heard my prayers, and that He loved me.

As she grew, everyone who met her was struck by her beauty, both inside and out. Strangers would stop me on the street, cooing over how lovely she was, and they always said the same thing: "She looks just like you." It took me a long time to accept that, to see that the beauty I saw in my daughter was a reflection of my own. But Imose taught me to see myself differently.

Through her, I began to heal from the wounds of my past.

Imose had a pure heart and an innocent obsession with

angels. She would ask me time and
again, "Mommy, when am I going to
see an angel? They're so beautiful!" I
used to tell her about the angels
mentioned in the Bible, and she was
captivated by the thought of seeing
one of these heavenly beings. Her
fascination with angels was like how

other little girls might be enchanted by unicorns or
rainbows, but for Imose, it was always angels.

After the tragedy, I was
haunted by the thought
that my daughters had
died alone. I couldn't bear
the idea that they were by
themselves in their final
moments. But in the midst

of my anguish, God assured me that they weren't alone—
that He had sent angels to be with them. This brought me a
measure of peace, knowing that even when I couldn't be
there, they were not forsaken, and Imose finally got to see
her angels. The scripture that says, "I will never leave you nor
forsake you," became a source of comfort for me. I clung to

the belief that God had not abandoned my girls, just as I hoped He had not abandoned me.

As time passed, I found it difficult to understand why this had happened, why God would allow such pain into my life. People often questioned my faith—"If God is so great, why did He take your children?" But faith doesn't always provide answers to the "why." Instead, it gives us the strength to move forward to the "what" and "how", even when the burden of loss feels unbearable. I didn't move on; I moved forward, carrying the love and the weight of losing my daughters. It took immense courage to open my heart again, to trust God with the lives of my new daughters, Ngozi and Nkiru. Trusting Him after such a loss was a slow and painful process, but it was necessary for healing.

In the years that followed, God continued to show me His grace. One of Imose's first-grade friends wrote about her in a college essay, describing how Imose had touched her life. When the time came for that class to graduate from Shaker Heights high school, I was honored to be their senior advisor. Seeing those first graders as young adults allowed me, in some small way, to imagine what Imose might have been like. At their graduation, they even arranged a moment of silence for Imose. It was a powerful reminder that her short life had left a lasting impact on those who knew her. In that moment I felt proud knowing that the lessons I instilled in Imose resonated to this day. I also felt the goodness of God, knowing that even in the midst of my pain, He was still working to bring something beautiful out of the ashes.

Imose was more than just my daughter; she was my teacher, my healer, my beautiful gift from God. She showed me that I was capable of loving deeply, that I was worthy of being loved, and that I could overcome the darkness of my past. Through her, I learned that true beauty comes not from what the world sees, but from the love and grace that we carry within us. As I moved through the days of mourning, thoughts of Chika, my second daughter, filled my heart. Her resilience and fiery personality stood in stark contrast to the quiet strength of Imose, and in her own way, Chika had been teaching me lessons of strength and survival. It was time to reflect on how Chika's presence shaped me.

CHAPTER 5: CHIKORA, MY FIRECRACKER OF RESILIENCE

Chikora. Her name means "God is greater than the community." Before she was even born, I knew that name would define her. I found it in the Igbo 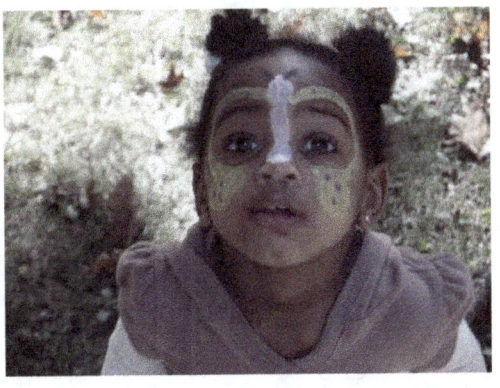 dictionary—a name reserved for a child born amidst controversy, a child destined to rise above judgment. And that's exactly what "Chika" was: a living testament to God's greatness, even when the world seemed set against us.

Chika came into my life during one of the most turbulent periods I've ever faced. I was married to Vincent, but the marriage was crumbling. We were in and out of marriage counseling, desperately trying to make things work. Deep down, I knew it was over. I wanted to stay for reasons that went beyond love—I wanted to help him stay in the country. Divorce would mean jeopardizing his chances. But eventually, I decided to leave. I moved into a two-bedroom apartment on Lakeshore Blvd. near Cleveland, and that was the beginning of a new chapter in my life.

It was during this time that I met Chukwuma. His mother was a client of mine, and as I helped her set up her home healthcare business, Chukwuma began to show up more and more frequently. One thing led to another, and soon I found myself in a relationship with him, even though I was still legally married. Six months later, I found out I was pregnant with Chika.

The pregnancy was far from easy. I was dealing with community gossip, divorce proceedings, and the emotional rollercoaster of a tumultuous relationship with Chukwuma. My mother-in-law, who was a nurse, even suggested I get an abortion. But I couldn't. I had the means to support my child on my own, and I knew I wanted to keep her. I named her

Chikora because, in my heart, I knew that God was greater than the community's judgment, greater than the controversy surrounding her birth.

Chika's pregnancy, much like her personality, was full of fire and resilience. Despite the emotional turmoil, she arrived the day before Thanksgiving—small but mighty, with a loud cry that filled the hospital nursery. She had a set of lungs on her, and I remember the nurses joking that they had to move her to a separate room because her cries were waking up all the other babies. From the moment she entered the world, Chika made sure she was heard.

Chukwuma left shortly after she was born, abandoning us to attend his brother's baby's baptism, a decision that left me heartbroken. But even in those lonely days, I found comfort in my bond with Chika. She was born into a world filled with controversy and chaos, but she thrived in it, teaching me how to hold my head high and not care what others thought. I was her protector, her mother, and she taught me that I didn't need anyone's approval. As long as I knew my worth and believed in what God said about me, I could face anything.

Chika had a vibrant personality. Even as a baby, she was a spitfire—observant and sharp beyond her years. At just one and a half, she could follow instructions like an adult. I'd tell her, "Chika, go upstairs and grab your baba," and she'd march up to her room, grab her bottle, and bring it back down like a little soldier. She was full of energy and determination, always finding ways to surprise me with her quick wit.

She had this hilarious habit of putting her hand up as if she was going to hit you, but when I'd say, "Chika, put your hand down," she'd do it. Then, as if to outsmart me, she'd lean against the wall, put  up her foot, and act like she was going to kick me instead. She was so full of life, always keeping me on my toes, always pushing the limits in her own mischievous way.

As she grew, Chika continued to be a force to be reckoned with. She loved dresses, but she was also a tomboy at heart, never afraid to dig in the dirt or march to the beat of her own drum. Her smile and spirit were contagious, and I often found myself in awe of her ability to be both loving and fiercely independent. I'd sometimes call her my "CEO" because I could already tell she was destined to run things. She reminded me so much of her little sister Nkiru, always showing signs of leadership and strength.

Chika wasn't much of a talker, though. She had her own way of communicating, often using two-word sentences like "eat, eat mommy." I remember those words vividly, especially after the tragedy. In the days following the fire, I couldn't bring myself to eat. Grief had stolen my appetite, and I felt like I couldn't put anything in my body. Then, one day, while sitting at the kitchen counter, I heard Chika's voice in my spirit: "Eat, eat, mommy." It was the first time I had eaten in days, and I knew she would want me to take care of myself, even if she wasn't there to remind me anymore.

Losing Chika, along with her sisters, broke me in ways I can hardly describe. But Chika's lesson to me was one of resilience. She taught me that no matter what the world says, no matter what circumstances you're born into, you define your own worth. She showed me that I no longer needed to be a people- pleaser, that I didn't have to live my life trying to earn the approval of others. I could stand tall in the knowledge that God's opinion of me mattered most, and that I was priceless in His eyes.

Chika was more than just my daughter—she was a mirror

reflecting my own strength back at me. She was my spitfire, my CEO, my lesson in resilience and self-worth. And while she may no longer be here physically, the lessons she taught me live on, guiding me through even the darkest of days. After Chika's passing, the weight of grief was unimaginable, but there was still one more daughter to remember. Anya, my youngest, had survived the fire for three days. Her spirit stayed with me, and the decision to donate her organs became a defining io9journey to find meaning in the midst of tragedy.

CHAPTER 6: ANYA, MY HEART THAT BEATS ON

Anyachiemeka
(pronounced "AHN-yah-CHEE-eh-MEH-kah"). Her name means "the eye of God has done well for me." She came into my life during a

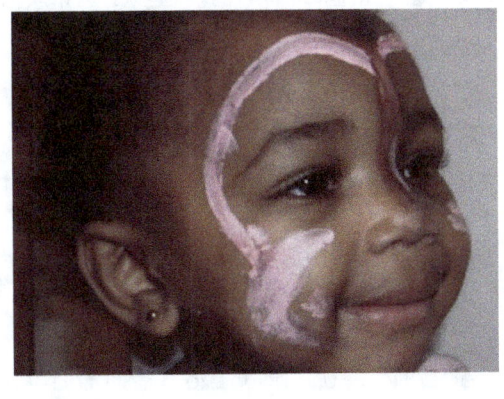

time of exhaustion and uncertainty, but from the moment I knew she was on the way, I was determined to do right by her. Anya was born just ten and a half months after Chika, making them what people often call "Irish twins." I had barely recovered from Chika's birth when I found out I was pregnant again, and physically, I was drained. Chukwuma and I decided to elope, much to the disapproval of his family.

Emotionally, however, the bond with Anya was immediate. Despite my exhaustion, I spent every night singing lullabies to her, just like I had done with her older sisters. My body may have been weary, but the love I felt for her was boundless. I would lie in bed, rocking her to sleep inside me, as I hummed the songs from Mellow My Baby, the same album I used with Imose and Chika. Over time, those quiet moments together strengthened our connection, and I found peace in knowing that she was already a part of me in more ways than one.

Anya's pregnancy was different from the others. I was busy raising two young children, and my marriage with my Chukwuma was already starting to fall apart due to his mother forcing him to decide between his family and his marriage. I felt immense pressure to maintain an image of perfection—to show the world that we were a happy family, that I had it all together. But the truth was, I was struggling. Behind closed doors, the abuse I endured during my pregnancy with Anya drained my spirit. I built walls to protect myself from the pain, all while trying to shield my children from the chaos around us.

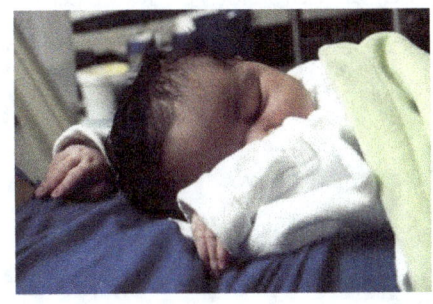

But even in the darkest moments, Anya gave me strength. Her name was more than just a name; it was a prayer, a declaration that despite everything, God had still done well for me. I held onto that belief, even when I felt like I was falling apart. I remember calling her my "cling-on", because she always clung to me. She never left my side, even before she was born.

When she finally arrived on October 7th, 2006, two days before my birthday, I looked at her and thought, "Whose baby is this?" She was so pale, with her tiny features, and for a moment, I was shocked. But as I studied her, I realized she looked exactly like my grandmother.

Not just in appearance, but in her gestures and movements. It was uncanny. My grandmother used to tilt her head to the side and raise her shoulder, and there was Anya, doing the same thing. Even more strangely, they shared the same thyroid condition. It was as if my grandmother had come back through Anya, a spiritual and physical connection that I couldn't deny. Anya had come into my life to teach me lessons that I wouldn't fully understand until much later.

Anya was a joy, always smiling, always eager to help. She had the biggest heart, and I mean that in every way. Even as a baby, she wanted to be with her older sisters, doing whatever they did. If I asked her to bring me something, she would run to fetch it with a grin on her face. I couldn't even go to the bathroom without her sticking her fingers underneath the door, just to let me know she was there. She

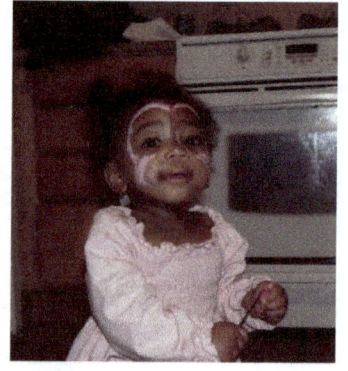

loved her macaroni and cheese—her favorite dish in the world. Every time I made it, she would light up. It's a memory that would later mean more to me than I ever could have imagined.

When the fire happened, I lost

Imose and Chika instantly, but Anya survived for three days. I can still remember the drive to the hospital, terrified of what I would find, praying and pleading with God to let her live. I had already lost two daughters, and I didn't think I could bear losing another. I was so desperate that at one point, I told God if Anya died, I wouldn't be able to go on. But in that moment of despair, the Holy Spirit spoke to me. It wasn't an audible voice, but a knowing deep inside me. "No devastation or pain will ever outshine my glory," I heard. And then, "Anya will live on."

I held onto that promise as I entered the hospital, convinced that Anya would survive. But when I saw her, struggling to breathe, her tiny chest rising and falling with effort, I realized her situation was far more dire than I had hoped. The doctors told me she wouldn't make it through the night, but my faith wouldn't let me believe that. I prayed over her, surrounded by family, asking God for a miracle. On the second day, a nurse showed me the burn pattern on her back—it looked like angel wings. I knew then that God was with us, but I still prayed for more time.

On the third day, I stood by Anya's bed, holding her hand, and that same voice came back to me: "It's time to let her go." At first, I refused to believe it. How could God tell me she would live on and then ask me to let her go? But then I realized what He meant. Her body had healed, but her brain was gone. And now, it was up to me to decide if she would live on through someone else.

The decision to donate Anya's organs wasn't easy, but it was clear. God had healed her in ways I hadn't expected. Her heart, lungs, and other organs were healthy. I knew that somewhere out there, another mother needed Anya's heart just as much as I did. And so, I made the decision to donate. I couldn't let another family go through the pain I was enduring if I could help prevent it.

A few months later, I received a letter from the family of the boy who received Anya's heart. The family was told that if he didn't receive a heart before Christmas that he would die. Anya's heart turned out to be their Christmas gift. His name was Gabriel, and his favorite food was also macaroni and cheese! When I read that, I broke down. It was as if Anya was sending me a message, telling me, "Mommy, I'm still here.

My heart is still beating on." That's when I knew she would live on, just as God had promised.

Anya taught me courage in the face of unimaginable loss. She showed me how to give, even when it hurts, and how to trust that God's plan is bigger than our own. I miss her every day, but I find comfort in knowing that through her, two other families were given miracles. On my worst day, I became someone else's greatest hope, and that is the economy of God. Anya may have only been with me for 14 months, but her life continues to make a difference in this world. She is, and will always be, my heart that beats on. As I processed the loss of all three of my daughters, the overwhelming grief settled in. I couldn't escape the weight of it, but I knew that surviving this kind of pain required more than just time—it required confronting the raw reality of my grief, every single day.

CHAPTER 7: A MOTHER'S GRIEF

The immediate shock of losing my girls after the fire felt like I was trapped in a never-ending nightmare. I didn't want to wake up. Only in my dreams, the girls were still there with me, alive and well. But every morning, waking up was a harsh reminder that they were gone. I didn't want to eat, and I couldn't fall asleep unless the lights were on. Even when I managed to sleep, the slightest noise woke me up. My body was in survival mode.

Shortly after the death of my girls, my immediate family arrived. When my then five-year-old niece Lazara walked into the hospital, my heart dropped. It was like I was seeing

Imose's ghost. Lazara's hair was braided much like Imose's hair. The resemblance was uncanny. At first it was hard being around her. I couldn't be around her. But over the next couple of days, her presence brought me comfort that I didn't know I needed. Once I got over the initial shock of the resemblance, I wouldn't let Lazara leave my side. She became a surrogate child to me, in memory of Imose.

In those early days, I survived minute by minute. It wasn't even about making it through the day—it was about getting through the next second, the next breath. My mind was constantly grappling with how to move forward. I went from caring for three beautiful little girls to being an empty nester overnight. It was surreal. I had been changing diapers, cooking meals, and managing a busy household, but suddenly everything stopped. I was lost in the stillness, the silence.

The physical symptoms of grief were overwhelming. It felt like my stomach had dropped, like that feeling you get on a roller coaster, but it never went away. I felt sick, cold, and empty, like someone had ripped my skin off and dipped me in salt water. The pain was sharp and heavy, suffocating at times. My body felt foreign to me, as if I had been drained of all energy.

The guilt consumed me. I kept replaying every decision in my mind, wondering what I could have done differently. I felt guilty that I wasn't there, guilty that I didn't make different choices. I kept thinking, "What if Imose had gone to her dad's house like she planned?" "What if I had stayed at home with the babies?" "What if we would've chosen a different house to move into?" "What if our babysitters have been older?" The weight of these thoughts crushed me, making the grief even more unbearable.

As the days turned into weeks and months, my grief shifted, but it was always there. I was diagnosed with complex grief which mirrors major depressive disorder. The only difference between complex and major is that I know the when and why my brain changed. I was also diagnosed with PTSD and trauma brain. I began taking medication just to manage the overwhelming sadness and anxiety. I cried a lot, but I never cried in front of others. I didn't want my grief to be too heavy for them. So, I would wait until I was alone to cry out in agony. It took years before I could sleep peacefully without medication.

The decision to leave my husband, Chukwuma, came a month after the fire. I couldn't handle the emotional abuse any longer. I was grieving the loss of my daughters, and I knew I couldn't take on anyone else's pain. I moved in with my friend Andrea, and I started to heal, but it was slow. I felt like I had lost everything—my girls and my marriage.

Prayer became my lifeline during that time. I would walk and pray, and when I needed to distract myself, I would turn to comedy. I remember watching the Saturday Night Live Christmas special, and for the first time in weeks, I laughed. It was a belly laugh, the kind that reminds you you're still alive, still capable of feeling joy, even if just for a moment. Watching comedians such as Chris Rock became a ritual for me. I didn't want anything serious or melodramatic—I just needed to laugh. That laughter was a reminder that I was still soft at my core, that I could still experience joy even in the midst of grief.

Communicating my grief to others was initially hard. I'm a direct communicator, so I would just tell people, "I'm struggling today. I'm on the struggle bus." Sometimes, I'd ask friends to meet me for coffee just so I could talk. People were compassionate and tried to understand, but no one could truly grasp what I was going through. There were moments when I felt completely isolated, even when surrounded by people.

My family and friends were my lifeline. My mom would stay

up with me at night, praying and talking to me when I couldn't sleep. She'd always say, "You're my baby, and my baby's hurting, so I'm hurting too." Their support meant everything to me, and I wouldn't have made it through without them.

My day-to-day routine changed drastically. I went from being busy all the time—taking the girls to Kinder Music, Little Gym, and other activities—to having nothing to do. My house was empty, and I didn't have to worry about cooking or taking care of anyone. The stillness was suffocating.

I was also angry. I was so angry at the unfairness of it all. Why did my girls have to die when there are parents out there who don't even want their children, who abuse them? It didn't make sense. But after some time I realized that it wasn't the children's fault that they were being abused, which helped me manage my anger. But the anger still there, lingering in the background.

Simple things, like going to the grocery store, triggered my grief the most. I would avoid grocery stores because every time I went, I'd be reminded of who wasn't there. I wasn't buying pull-ups, diapers, or their favorite snacks anymore. That reminder was too painful, so I just stopped going. Eventually, I could only shop at stores I had never taken the girls to, just to avoid the memories.

The dreams of my daughters helped me through the grief. Two weeks before Imose passed, she told me she wanted to give her life to Christ and be baptized. I hold on to that memory because it brings me comfort. I also had a dream about her after she passed. In the dream, I was driving around, running errands with the girls. I looked in the backseat and saw Imose sitting between the two babies, smiling at me. She said, "Mommy, I'm okay." That dream reassured me that her spirit was at peace, and it still brings me comfort to this day.

Faith was my constant companion during those early days. I listened to praise and worship music over and over, especially from the International House of Prayer in Kansas City. I would read the Psalms and meditate on them, and the song Never Would Have Made It by Marvin Sapp became my anthem. Even though I was angry with God, I knew I needed Him to survive this. My faith was the reason I made it through.

Grief is a long, complicated journey. There were days when it felt impossible to move forward, but I prayed my way out of bed. Even on the days when the only thing I could do was get dressed, that was a triumph. My girls were gone, but I was still alive. I had to keep going. But it wasn't just my grief over my daughters that I had to confront. My marriage, already strained before the fire, began to unravel. The loss of our children magnified the cracks that had long existed, pushing us both to a breaking point.

CHAPTER 8: DISSOLUTION

The truth is my marriage was deteriorating long before the tragedy. The fire just ignited the inevitable. About a month after the girls died, Chukwuma and I separated. He was angry—not just about the loss of our daughters, but about my belief in God. He couldn't understand why I continued to pray and hold onto my faith when, in his eyes, God had failed us. I couldn't argue with him because, in some ways, I felt the same. But I knew I had to hold onto the little piece of God that had sustained me through my life.

Chukwuma gave me an ultimatum—either him or God. I chose God.

My feelings of isolation contributed to the breakdown of our marriage. I felt utterly alone. Chukwuma couldn't understand the depths of my grief, and I couldn't understand his. He buried himself in work, coding, and smoking pot, while I threw myself into prayer and rebuilding the house. On the outside, we might have seemed physically present, but inside, we were both distant—living in two different worlds of grief.

Chukwuma and I briefly reconciled. After I moved out and stayed with my friend Andrea, Chukwuma kept calling, begging for forgiveness and saying he had made a mistake by asking me to choose between him and God. I loved Chukwuma. I didn't love how he treated me, but I couldn't bear one more loss in my life. So I went back to him, hoping things would be different. I wanted to believe he had changed, that we could start anew. But it wasn't long before I realized I had stepped back into the same abusive cycle.

We got back together right around Easter, and a month later, I found out on Mother's Day that I was pregnant with our daughter Ngozi. We were both excited, and for a while, things felt right. Chukwuma suggested we renew our vows, and I poured myself into planning a vow renewal while figuring out how to rebuild our house.

The isolation I felt wasn't just emotional; it was also deeply spiritual. I didn't have anyone who could truly understand what I was going through. There was no one who could walk with me through the unique loss of my daughters. That loneliness was cold and empty, and it drove a wedge further between Chukwuma and I. While I turned to faith, Chukwuma withdrew further, losing himself in his own despair.

Our grief manifested in completely different ways. I cried and prayed, seeking solace in God and the church. I began to eat excessively, trying to fill the void that grief had left. It wasn't long before I gained so much weight that I reached 404 pounds. Food became the only thing that felt safe, the only thing that didn't hurt me emotionally. Meanwhile, Chukwuma worked nonstop, throwing himself into his job, repeating that "someone has to pay the bills" since I wasn't able to work.

In December of 2008, a year and ten days after the fire, I gave birth to Ngozichukwunyere (pronounced "Nn-GO-zee-CHOO-koo-NYE-reh"), whose name means "the blessing of God has returned back to me." She was six weeks premature and my only birth that was a c-section, due to her being wrapped in her umbilical cord. It felt like a moment of redemption, a glimmer of hope after so much loss. But just a mere two weeks later, I found myself in the hospital on Christmas Day. I wasn't feeling well, and when I asked

Chukwuma to take me to the hospital, he told me to drive myself since I just two weeks earlier gave birth. I was in no shape to drive, but I did. When the doctors ran tests, they found a severe infection and what they initially thought was pancreatic cancer. I vividly remember the doctor walking into the room and leaning over saying "we see a thickening around your liver."

I'll never forget the terror of hearing that diagnosis, but something inside me knew it wasn't true. I told the doctors they were wrong, that God wouldn't give me a new baby just to take me away with cancer. After further tests, they discovered I had a pheochromocytoma (fee-oh-kroh-moh-sy-TOH-muh), a rare tumor connected to my adrenal gland. The tumor had caused all my complications during pregnancies, including preeclampsia (pree-ih-KLAMP-see-uh). That diagnosis saved my life.

As I recovered from surgery, I noticed Chukwuma becoming more distant. He later admitted he was terrified—he thought he was going to lose me like we had lost our daughters. He couldn't bear the thought of raising a new baby alone. That fear manifested in control and possessiveness. He wanted to keep us safe; to control everything around us so he wouldn't lose anything else. But that control turned into abuse, both verbal and physical.

Eventually, I couldn't take it anymore. After all the emotional abuse, the threats, and the isolation, I decided to leave for good when Chukwuma threatened to kill me. I knew then that I had to save myself and my daughters from further harm.

Our marriage, already weakened by years of grief and unresolved issues, crumbled under the weight of all we had been through. I had given everything I could to make it work, but it wasn't enough. I realized that healing had to start with me, that I couldn't save Chukwuma or fix our broken marriage on my own.

Grief, abuse, and trauma had taken their toll. It wasn't just about losing my daughters anymore—it was about losing myself. Leaving the marriage was a necessary step toward reclaiming my life, my faith, and my healing. It was the end of one chapter and the beginning of another—one where I could focus on myself and my children without the constant fear and turmoil that had defined our relationship. Amidst the dissolution of my marriage, I found a glimmer of hope in the most unexpected place—organ donation. Anya's gift to others became my way of finding light in the darkness, showing me that even through loss, life could continue.

CHAPTER 9: ANYA'S HEART AND THE GIFT OF LIFE

About a year after Anya passed, I was invited to share my story on a panel with LifeBanc, the organ and tissue donation organization. It was an opportunity to honor my daughters by talking about why I chose to donate Anya's organs. Every time I told our story, it felt like I was keeping their memory alive. Making the decision to donate Anya's organs was one of

the most significant parts of my grieving process—it allowed me to find light in the midst of so much darkness. Knowing that two other families were able to enjoy more time with their loved ones because of Anya's gift helped lift some of the burden I carried.

I didn't struggle with the decision to donate Anya's organs. From the moment I was asked, I knew it was the right thing to do. It was a decision made from a place of clarity, even in the midst of chaos. Deep down, I knew that helping someone else was what I was supposed to do. If I had been in their shoes, I would have hoped for someone to say yes to me.

Anya's donation gave me a sense of purpose. It allowed me to share the gift of life with others, even in the face of death. Knowing that another child was out there—eating macaroni and cheese, running, laughing, and living— because Anya's heart gave me peace. In the midst of my pain, another family was experiencing joy.

I've always believed that once we leave this world, we no longer need our bodies—our "earth suits," as I call them. I tell my surviving daughters, Ngozi and Nkiru, that while we're here, we must take care of our earth suits. But once we're gone, we don't need them anymore—someone else might. My daughters didn't need their bodies any longer, but other families did. That gave me strength. It's why I felt so strongly about donation.

There's a misconception, particularly in the African American community, that organ donation conflicts with our faith. For me, there was no conflict at all. The Bible says that when we leave this body, it returns to dust, and we receive a glorified body. So why not help someone else in the process? I knew I had to be an advocate for this cause, to represent for African Americans, people of faith, and parents who have lost children but still find hope in donation.

Faith influenced my decision at every step. I understood that everything we have—our bodies, our gifts— can be used for something greater. Anya's heart had a new purpose, a new life to fulfill. I said yes to organ donation because I knew it was God's plan, and that gave me peace.

One of the most powerful moments for me came when I met a heart recipient who had received a heart from an 18-year-old. He asked if I wanted to listen to his heartbeat, and I immediately said yes. The sound of that heart beating inside someone else's body was a reminder of the incredible gift Anya had given. It brought me joy to know her heart was still out there, living on.

Anya's heart holds a deep significance for me. When the

doctors first reviewed her records, they didn't think her heart could be used. She had been without oxygen for nearly eight minutes after the fire, and her heart had stopped. But the firefighters worked tirelessly, even knowing my other two daughters wouldn't survive, and they got Anya's heart beating again. By the time she reached the hospital, she was brain dead, but her heart was miraculously restored. Three days later, the doctors told me her heart was one of the healthiest they had ever seen. It was God's touch. Her heart was healed in those three days, just as God had promised—Anya would live on.

The donation of Anya's organs not only saved lives, but it also saved me. It was a gift for my heart, a light in my pain. Through her, I found a way to keep moving forward, knowing her life had touched others. I continued to advocate for organ and tissue donation in her honor. I served on the LifeBanc board for  eight years and the Donate Life National Board for two. In 2012, Anya was honored at the Rose Bowl Parade on the Donate Life float, with her face beautifully made from organic materials. Her legacy lives on in the work I do.

Healing has been a long journey. Just like Anya's heart was healed in those three days, my own healing took many years. I learned that grief isn't something you "get over"—it's something you go through.

Healing can come in many forms, and for me, it was knowing that Anya's heart gave another family six more years with their child. When I found out that her heart recipient had passed away, I grieved for that family. But I also felt joy knowing Anya's heart had given them six more birthdays, six more Christmases, and countless memories. That's a gift I will always treasure.

Organ and tissue donation has changed how I see life and loss. It taught me that life is precious, and death is part of it. Living fully means accepting that one day, we will all face death, but in the meantime, we can make choices that leave a lasting impact. We can create hope for others, even in the darkest of times.

My daughters' legacies live on through the causes I champion in their names—Anya through organ and tissue donation, Imose through arts programs, and Chika through women's empowerment. No life is too short to make a difference. Anya's heart showed me that even a 14-month-old can be a hero. And because of her, on my worst day, two other families received their greatest miracle. That's the beauty of life and loss—the pain and joy are intertwined, but through it all, hope endures. But even with that hope, my faith was deeply tested. I couldn't understand why God had taken my children, and the questions I asked were heavy with doubt and anger. It was in this questioning that my faith was truly tested, and ultimately, strengthened.

CHAPTER 10: FAITH TESTED, FAITH STRENGTHENED

My faith underwent a seismic shift after the loss of my daughters. Before the tragedy, faith was something I carried with me, something that was always present, but perhaps not fully tested. After the fire, it became the foundation I clung to, the only thing that could possibly help me navigate through the chaos and devastation. My faith evolved—becoming deeper, more concrete, and less superficial. It wasn't just a belief; it was something I needed to prove to myself. If God was real, then He would be able to get me through this.

I wasn't afraid to ask God the hard questions, and I wasn't going to keep those questions unspoken. I needed to challenge God, to question why I had to go through such unimaginable pain. There were moments of pure frustration, where I felt like I was in a love-hate relationship with God. My faith stretched from a level one to what felt like a level ten billion. I had to believe God for the impossible because everything around me seemed hopeless. My daughters were gone, my marriage was falling apart, and everything I had built was in shambles. I couldn't see God, but I had to trust that He was still there, guiding me, even when I couldn't feel His presence.

One of the most pivotal moments that challenged my faith was losing all my children. After I made the decision to donate Anya's organs, I was left with the crushing question: Why did all my children have to die? Couldn't I have been left with just one? But the voice inside asked me, "Which one would you have chosen?" I couldn't answer that question because I loved them all equally. It was then that I realized I couldn't harbor anger toward God for their deaths. It took me a long time to forgive myself, especially for asking Imose to stay that night. I carried guilt for a long time, believing that maybe her staying put her in harm's way.

The end of my marriage was another blow that tested my faith. Why did something else have to die? Why couldn't this part of my life survive either? Seeing news stories about parents who abused their children—parents who still had their kids while I had lost mine—made me question God. I wasn't a bad mother; I loved my children deeply. So why did they have to die? Was I being punished for something in my past? Was there something flawed in me?

My anger toward God manifested in ways that surprised even me. I prayed, but I was also deeply angry. It felt like being a child who was mad at their parent, hitting them while still clinging to them. I was so mad at God for allowing this to happen. I had experienced God's love before, so why would He let something so horrific happen to me? What was I supposed to learn from this immense pain? Could there have been another way? My frustration grew as I realized that this was no surprise to God—He knew this was going to happen, and He didn't stop it.

My anger didn't just stay between me and God; it spilled over into my interactions with others. If someone messed up my coffee order, it was like an excuse to unleash all the rage and grief inside me. Anger felt good—it allowed me to release the deep pain that was festering. But beneath that anger was a broken heart, a heart that was hurting in ways that no one could soothe—not even God.

Despite all my doubts and anger, praise and gratitude became my lifeline. I remember a few days after Anya passed, God told me to find something to be grateful for. So, I did. I started practicing gratitude daily. Even when everything seemed to be falling apart, I was thankful that I was still in my right mind, that I knew who I was, and that I could feel. The fact that I could feel pain was a reminder that I was still alive.

My family, my community, and prayer kept me going. Music, especially praise and worship, ministered to my spirit when nothing else could.

Prayer became more than a ritual; it became my connection to God. It was how I released my rage, how I settled my mind, and how I found peace. In those moments of intimate dialogue with God, I was brutally honest about my feelings. Sometimes, I didn't even talk—I just sat in silence, meditating for hours, contemplating the journey ahead.

Through all of this, I questioned why life had to be so painful. Why do we have to endure such intense suffering to experience joy? Why do parents have to bury their children?

And more than anything, I questioned why God didn't intervene. But over time, I realized those weren't the questions I should be asking. The real questions were: What do I do next? How do I move forward? How do I keep from getting stuck in bitterness? How do I love again, trust again, and live without fear?

In the end, I bet on God. I put all my faith in Him, even though I was angry, even though I had doubts. I knew that there was no one else, no other force that could get me through this but God. And while I thought I would walk away from God once the pain subsided; I never did. To this day, I trust Him with both the seen and unseen, knowing that faith, even in the darkest moments, is the only way forward.

My religious community played a complicated role in my journey. While their support was well- intentioned, I also received some very bad theology. People tried to rationalize the tragedy by telling me that I wasn't "equally yoked" with my husband or that I was being punished for mistakes I made in my youth. If I didn't have my own understanding of God's love and grace, I might have turned away from Him entirely. But I knew too much about God's unmerited grace to believe those lies. So, while the community tried to help, in the end, it was me and God—working through the pain together.

Prayer, music, and meditation carried me through this time of grief. I found solace in praise and worship, in the quiet moments of reflection, and in the strength I found when I let go of anger. God's presence, even in the midst of devastation, was real. It was that faith that kept me going when everything else fell apart. As I continued to wrestle with faith, grace slowly emerged. It didn't come all at once, but with each step forward, I began to feel its presence, guiding me toward healing. It was time to embrace the grace that had carried me this far.

CHAPTER 11: GRACE IN HEALING

After the tragedy, my relationship with God was reshaped, growing from something distant to a deeply personal and transformative experience. Before the fire, God felt like a mystery—a force I revered but didn't truly know. After losing my daughters, that distance vanished. God became real, raw, and close. I wasn't just praying anymore—I was wrestling with Him, demanding answers, and unwilling to accept empty platitudes. My pain drove me to seek understanding, and grace gave me the courage to pursue God relentlessly.

One defining moment was the rebuild of our home. After the fire, the insurance only covered basic repairs, leaving us with limited resources. The structure itself needed repairs, and I didn't think I could live there again. But I began to dream, asking God what changes would make the house livable again. The foyer, where Imose died, needed to be different. The window where the babysitters jumped had to be rebuilt. I prayed and even drew sketches, not knowing how we'd afford it.

One Sunday, God pushed me to go to church, where I met a missionary who suggested involving trade unions to help rebuild. That suggestion became a blessing. With their help, I became the general manager of the rebuild, overseeing every step while carrying the weight of grief. I had to rebuild my home while rebuilding myself. I was pregnant with Nkiruka which means "God's future is greater" at the time, and my goal was to bring her home to a house that would feel safe—both physically and emotionally.

Each day at the house was like watching my life being reconstructed. One moment stood out: when a carpenter revealed that the original house, built in 1910, had serious structural integrity issues. It had been standing on one beam where three were required. Stripping the house down to its core allowed us to fix what had been unseen for years, preventing another potential tragedy. I realized that I, too, had been holding myself up with spiritual weakness beneath the surface. The fire, though devastating, exposed areas in my life that needed rebuilding—from the inside out. God wasn't just rebuilding the house; He was healing me.

As previously mentioned, I had ballooned to 404 pounds, feeding my emotions rather than feeling them. I knew I had to make a change, not just for myself but for Nkiru and Ngozi. I started walking, initially as a way to honor Anya's memory through a 5K walk for organ donation. That walk became a turning point. I wasn't just walking off the physical weight; I was shedding the spiritual burdens that had weighed me down since the fire. Walking became part of my healing, each step a testament to the grace that was slowly mending my soul.

I eventually participated in 5Ks, 10Ks, and even marathons, running the ages of each of my daughters on their birthdays: 12 miles for Imose, 9 for Chika, and 8 for Anya. On December 1st of that year, I ran 27 miles—the combined ages of my girls—completing my first marathon and ultra-marathon in their memory. With each mile, I felt like I was reclaiming pieces of myself.

Grace allowed me to forgive myself for the perceived failures as a mother and wife. It wasn't easy, but I learned that grace and forgiveness are inseparable. I had to extend grace to myself before I could offer it to others. Only then could I begin to heal.

My daughters' legacy lives on, not just in my heart but through the work I do—whether it's speaking about organ donation, participating in charitable walks, or simply sharing my story. They are the reason for everything I do. I feel their presence often. There was a time I was asleep on the couch and felt a tap on my shoulder, thinking it was one of my younger daughters. But when I checked, they were both sound asleep. In that moment, I knew it was Chika watching over me.

In other moments, I've heard the girls' laughter or seen them in dreams where they tell me everything will be okay. These encounters remind me that life continues beyond what we see, and my daughters are still very much a part of this world, watching over us.

Parenting Ngozi and Nkiru after losing their sisters has been incredibly difficult. I've had to manage my grief while helping them navigate their young lives. I admit that at times, I parented out of guilt, trying to compensate for what we all lost. But I've always made sure they know about their sisters. We celebrate their birthdays, and we talk about them often. It's important to me that their memories stay alive, not just for me but for Ngozi and Nkiru too. They are part of a family that spans this world and the next.

To parents who have lost children, my heart breaks for you. I wish I could take your pain away, but know this: joy will return. It may seem distant, but it will come. You will laugh again. You will feel light again. It's like losing a limb—you never fully recover, but you learn to live with it. And you will survive.

Grace and hope are what carry you through. Give yourself permission to grieve, to hurt, and to heal. And know that one day, you will be reunited with your children in a place of endless joy. With grace came the opportunity to embrace life again. My daughters were gone, but their legacy lived on in everything I did. With their memories as my guide, I began to live with purpose, honoring them in every step I took.

CHAPTER 12: EMBRACING LIFE WITH PURPOSE

My life now, years after the loss of my daughters, is what I call a "wonderful hot mess." I tell people that I'm a hot mess that God is turning into a holy message. And despite all that's happened, I am living life to the fullest. But make no mistake, when my daughters died, I died too. A part of me left this world with them that day. So, in many ways, I am only 17 years old—post-trauma years. That's how I think of it. After the fire, I had to learn how to walk again, not physically, but spiritually and emotionally. I had to learn how to crawl, how to think at higher levels, and how to go deeper into my understanding of life and faith. I have what I refer to as "post-traumatic growth". It's the strength and resilience that I built after going through my trauma.

Nothing in life has been easy since then, but I've accepted that. Life is not a bowl of cherries. Every day brings new challenges, and I face them afraid, but I face them knowing that everything will work out. I have this eternal optimism that grew from my experience with loss. It's a belief that whatever you focus on becomes real. If I believe that the world is hostile, dangerous, and treacherous, then that's what it becomes for me. But if I choose to believe that the world is filled with love, despite its challenges, and that doing what is right—loving my neighbor and doing no harm—will lead to good outcomes, then that becomes my reality.

Since my daughters' passing, my purpose in life has evolved. I now live for three other human beings who are no longer here. I still have this incredible gift called life, and I refuse to squander it by feeling sorry for myself. Even if I never help another person in my lifetime, just getting out of bed each day and facing the world in my right mind is an accomplishment in itself. Before my daughters died, I wanted to be successful; I wanted to be a great mom. Now, my only goal is to make sure that I don't die with my gifts still inside me.

I often say that the richest places on Earth are not gold

mines or diamond mines, but graveyards. Too many people die without ever realizing their gifts, their talents, or their purpose. And I'll be damned if I let myself die with my gifts and purpose unfulfilled. I'm determined to live out my purpose, whether in small or big ways. Everything I'm meant to do, I want to do.

After the fire, I took on new roles to serve my community and honor my daughters. I became a community chaplain because I knew there were people who had been hurt by organized religion, who would never set foot in a church again. But they still needed someone to guide them spiritually. I call them the "nones" and the "dones"—people with no religious background or those who are completely done with organized religion. They want a pastor, someone to listen to them, to help them connect with their spiritual selves. I became that person for many. I help people grow spiritually, to deepen their relationship with the divine, even if it's outside of traditional religion.

I also became a teacher, obtaining my teaching license so I could be a light in schools. I wanted to connect with students across the city, to understand their needs, and to be someone they could rely on. Education became a way for me to stay connected to the community's heartbeat and pulse, to continue my daughters' legacy through service.

To honor my daughters, I found causes that reflected their spirits. I became involved with organ and tissue donation for Anya, arts programs for Imose, and women's empowerment initiatives for Chika. Through these causes, I've been able to keep their memories alive and find a sense of purpose. It's how I continue to make a difference on their behalf, even though they're not physically here with me.

My personal healing practices have also been essential. Prayer, mindfulness, meditation, and rest have kept me grounded. I find solace in music, gratitude, and journaling. These practices have helped me continue healing, even years after the loss. Faith, for me, is about believing in something you can't always see or touch, but it's not blind faith. My faith is eyes wide open. I've seen unimaginable devastation, but I still believe. I still have hope for the future.

One thing I've learned is that faith is a process. Just like building muscle, you start with small weights— small challenges—and over time, you grow stronger. Faith is no different. The more you go through, the stronger your faith becomes. But faith, like healing, requires going through something, not avoiding it. My faith is strong because I've seen the depths of despair and still chose to believe.

Giving back to the community has also been a major part of my healing. I speak about mental health, organ donation, and girls' empowerment. I mentor others who are grieving, offering love and support as they navigate their own loss. I make sure they know they're not alone, that there is still hope, even when it feels impossible.

Hope, for me, is like oxygen. It saved my life when Anya survived for those three days after the fire, and it continues to save me now. Hope allows me to look at my present circumstances and know that things won't always be this way. It's the lifeline I cling to during my darkest days.

Balancing the memory of my daughters with creating a new life for myself has been a delicate dance. I don't stay in the past; I move forward, but I carry my girls with me. They are still very present in my life. I remember them as the young women they would be today—17 years older. And in my heart, I honor them by living a life that is full of purpose, love, and grace.

CHAPTER 13: RADICAL FORGIVENESS AND THE JOURNEY TO GRACE

Forgiveness is a journey, not a destination. It's not something you achieve and then leave behind, but a daily decision—a practice of choosing to let go, again and again. For a long time after the fire, forgiveness felt impossible. I was angry. I was angry with myself, with others, and even with God. I had to process layers of emotions before I could even consider what forgiveness would look like in my life.

One of the hardest parts of my journey was forgiving myself. I carried a deep sense of guilt because, on that fateful night, I was the one who asked Imose to stay home. If I had just let her go to her dad's house as planned, she wouldn't have been there. It haunted me. I would replay that decision over and over in my mind, torturing myself with the "what ifs." The weight of self-blame was crushing, and for a while, I couldn't see a way out of it. I had to face the reality that, no matter how much I wished to turn back time, I couldn't change what happened. I had to forgive myself.

It took years to come to that place of self-forgiveness. I had to understand that, at the time, I made the best decision I could with the information I had. I didn't know what would happen. If I had, I would have gladly laid down my own life to save my girls. But hindsight is a tricky thing—it loves to torment you with the impossible. Through therapy, prayer, and the grace of God, I slowly learned to release that burden. Forgiveness, I realized, isn't about forgetting. It's about learning to cope with the pain and still choosing to move forward.

Forgiving others was just as difficult. I harbored a lot of anger toward the babysitters. They survived. They made it out of the fire alive while my daughters didn't. I couldn't understand how they could have left the house without my girls. In my mind, it seemed unthinkable, and for a long time, I wrestled with that. But, over time, I came to realize that they were young, terrified, just like anyone would be in such a traumatic situation. They did what they thought was best in a moment of chaos. Holding on to anger wasn't going to bring my girls back. It was only going to keep me stuck in that night forever.

I've also had to forgive those who were indifferent to my pain—people who didn't understand the weight I was carrying or who continued with their lives as if nothing had happened. That was a hard pill to swallow. I had to accept that while my world had stopped, the world around me kept spinning. People didn't feel the same loss I did, and that's not their fault. Forgiving them allowed me to stop expecting others to carry my pain. This was my burden, my journey, and I had to walk it without expecting others to feel what I was feeling.

But perhaps the most complex part of my forgiveness journey has been forgiving God. I was furious. Furious that He allowed this to happen. Furious that, as a mother, I wasn't able to protect my children. If God is all-knowing, why didn't He intervene? Why didn't He save them? Those were the questions that kept me up at night. I've always believed in God's plan, but this? This was too much. For a while, I held on to that fury, clinging to God with one hand

and shaking my fist at Him with the other.

However, in the quiet moments, I heard His voice. It wasn't the booming voice of certainty, but a whisper—a reminder that His plan is bigger than mine. I realized that even though I didn't understand why this happened, I needed God more than ever. Holding on to anger would only separate me from the one source of love and healing I had left. Forgiving God didn't mean I suddenly understood or accepted everything. It meant surrendering my need for answers and trusting that there was a bigger picture I couldn't yet see.

Over time, my relationship with God has deepened. The God I knew before the fire and the God I know now are not the same. My faith has evolved, moving from a place of rigid certainty to one of open acceptance. I no longer expect God to explain everything to me or give me just what I want. I've come to understand that faith is about trusting in God's love, even when it doesn't make sense. Radical forgiveness, for me, is about accepting that life is unfair, that bad things happen, and that we can't control everything. But in the midst of it all, God's grace is still there, holding us up.

This process has also taught me the importance of boundaries. Forgiveness doesn't mean allowing toxic people back into your life. It doesn't mean ignoring the pain they caused. It means releasing the hold that anger and bitterness have on you. I've learned to forgive while keeping my distance. I can forgive someone without restoring the relationship, and that's okay. Forgiveness doesn't mean weakness; it means wisdom. Wisdom to know when to let go and walk away. It means choosing peace over bitterness and setting healthy boundaries for your own well-being.

As I reflect on my journey of forgiveness, I realize how transformative it has been. Forgiveness has allowed me to move forward, to live fully, and to find joy again. It has freed me from the chains of anger and guilt and opened me up to love—radical love, the kind of love that sees beyond the pain and reaches for healing. And that's what grace is. It's loving, even when it's hard. It's forgiving, even when you don't understand. It's choosing peace, even when the storm is raging around you.

Every day, I make the choice to forgive. It's not a one-time thing; it's a daily practice. But in that practice, I've found a strength I didn't know I had. I've learned that forgiveness is not for the other person—it's for me. It's for my healing, my peace, and my future. And that's how I honor my girls—by choosing to live with grace, every single day.

CHAPTER 14: LIVING WITH GRACE

Living with grace after unimaginable loss has been a journey of learning, relearning, and letting go. Grace isn't something you earn; it's something you give. In the beginning, I thought of grace as a transaction—if you gave me grace, I would return it. But over the years, grace has transformed into something much deeper for me. It's about giving others grace, not because they deserve it, but because we are all made of the same dust. Grace is understanding that we are all human, prone to mistakes, and we all need compassion to navigate through life.

The hardest lesson in grace has been with myself. Losing my daughters left me shattered, and in those early years, I was harder on myself than anyone else could have been. I felt like I had failed them. But grace has taught me to soften those edges, to allow myself the space to feel, to grieve, and to heal. Grace is knowing when to push yourself forward and when to let yourself rest.

What I've learned is that you can't live with hate in your heart and still walk in grace. Hate was the closest emotion to what I felt when I lost my girls. Every time anger and hate reared their ugly heads, they took me to a dark place—a place I never want to return to. That's why I choose to err on the side of grace. It doesn't mean I ignore the pain or forget the wrongs done, but I refuse to allow hate to take root in my heart.

In practicing grace, I've also embraced humility. It's not about humiliation or feeling less than, but about recognizing that we all make mistakes. We all mess up. Holding someone else to a standard higher than I would hold for myself is not grace. Grace understands that, just like me, others are trying to navigate their own struggles.

One of the most profound moments of grace for me came after the girls died. It was during Easter, one of my favorite holidays. Growing up, Easter was a big deal in our household, and it was a special time for my girls and me. But after their passing, every reminder of Easter—every pastel dress, every basket of eggs—became a trigger. I remember walking into a store and breaking down because I could no longer shop for Easter dresses for my girls.

I pleaded with God, sitting in the dressing room, tears streaming down my face, asking why I couldn't even do something as simple as buy an Easter dress. And in that moment, I felt a shift. It was as if God was speaking directly to me, reminding me that my girls were in heaven, lacking nothing. They didn't need an Easter dress; they had everything they could ever need with Him. I realized then that everything I was feeling was about me—about what I had lost, not what they had gained.

I lost my children, but I didn't lose my mind. That moment of grace was life-changing for me. It wasn't just about letting go of the pain but about realizing that grace can transform your grief into something powerful. After that, I began buying Easter outfits for my niece and nephew and children in my church who didn't have them. If I couldn't be a mother to my girls, I would be a mother to the world. That's what grace did for me—it shifted my focus from my own pain to the needs of others.

Living with grace also means carrying my daughters with me, but not in the way you might think. I don't hold onto the memory of them as little girls. Over the years, I've allowed them to grow in my mind. I imagine who they would be today. I picture Imose at 23, Anya at 18, and Chika at 19. Their spirits have grown with me. This has helped me stay present in my life, especially with their younger sisters, Ngozi and Nkiru.

When I'm with my girls today, I'm reminded that grace is ongoing. Raising teenagers is no easy feat, and I often find myself thinking back to what I was like at their age. I remind myself to give them grace, just as I give myself grace. I'm not just trying to be a good mother; I'm trying to mother them in a way that allows them to grow into who they're meant to be.

Grace has been the thread that ties everything together—my grief, my healing, my faith. It has taught me that life is not perfect, that bad things happen to good people, and that sometimes, all you can do is trust in something greater than yourself. My faith today is nothing like it was before. Back then, it was soft and sweet, filled with promises of a perfect life if only I prayed hard enough. But life doesn't work that way. My faith now is gritty, real. It's the kind of faith that says, "Even in the darkest of times, I will still trust."

Grace and faith walk hand in hand. Grace is what has

allowed me to keep going, and faith is what has guided me. God has been my constant, the source of my strength. He's shown me time and again that even when I feel like I can't bear another day, He is there, holding me up, reminding me that I am not alone.

CONCLUSION: RISING FROM THE ASHES

As I look back on the events that have shaped my life, I realize that everything was a part of a larger journey, a process of learning and growth that I couldn't fully understand at the time. I've always felt that our lives on this earth are not accidents. I believe we choose the path we want to walk, the lessons we want to learn, and the people we want to journey with. This planet, this life, is a school, and each of us is here to learn profound lessons—compassion, empathy, resilience, love, and hope. We don't choose the specific events, but we choose to be part of the broader learning.

I had a vision during my sophomore year of college, where I was taken through someone's life. It was a dream, but one that left me with an indescribable sense of anguish and hope. In the dream, I saw myself speaking to a massive audience, declaring, "Back then I felt I was only worth a dollar, but now I know that I am priceless." It was years later that I understood the dream was a premonition—a glimpse of the trials I would face and the strength I would find in the aftermath. God was showing me that no matter how devastated I felt, I would come out on the other side, stronger and more valuable than I had ever imagined.

The loss of my three daughters was the most profound tragedy of my life, but it was also the beginning of my path toward healing and purpose. There's no way I could have known at the time that God was preparing me to rise from the ashes, but now I see that every step of my journey was leading me to this moment.

In the years since their passing, I've learned that healing is not automatic; it's a choice. It's a choice to get up each day, to live, to keep moving forward even when everything inside of you tells you to give up. God didn't give me the gift of life so that I could lay down and feel sorry for myself. My daughters—Imose, Chika, and Anya—may no longer be physically with me, but their spirit lives on, and their legacy continues to shape the person I am today. I live not only for myself but for them.

Through my experiences, I've come to understand that there is a power beyond what we can see, feel, or touch—a force that carries us through tragedy, heartache, and pain. This power is what kept me going when I wanted to give up. It's what reminded me, again and again, that I had a purpose, even when I didn't know what that purpose was.

My healing journey has been multifaceted. I've had to address my pain emotionally, physically, and spiritually. I found comfort in unexpected places—through touch therapy, nature walks, journaling, prayer, and music. I've learned that the body truly does keep the score. The pain I carried wasn't just emotional; it was stored deep within my body, and I had to work to release it. But through it all, God has been my guide, leaving me little breadcrumbs along the way—through dreams, through people, through His word—to remind me of who I am and why I am here.

At the heart of everything I do is the desire to bring light and hope to others. Whether I'm teaching, serving as a chaplain, or simply sharing my story, my purpose is to help people heal. We're not here alone. We're connected to something far greater than ourselves, and it's that connection that gives us the strength to keep going, no matter how heavy the burden may feel.

My daughters' lives were short, but their impact is everlasting. They journeyed with me for as long as they could, and for that, I am forever grateful. Their sacrifice, their lessons, and their love are embedded in everything I do. I honor them by living my life to the fullest, by helping others, and by never giving up.

Healing is hard work. It's not a linear process, and it doesn't happen overnight. But I believe that if we choose to rise from the ashes of our pain, we can find a strength we never knew we had. And in that strength, we can find ourselves and our purpose.

AFTERWARD

As I come to the end of this deeply personal journey, I find myself reflecting on the immense power of love, loss, and grace. Writing Good Grief, Great Grace has been both a painful and healing process, but one that I knew had to be done. I also knew that I couldn't go back and stay long in the past. I had to keep this process timed and measured, to reduce the emotions that occur when revisiting such a painful place in my life. This book represents not just the story of my daughters and the tragedy that forever changed my life, but also the incredible grace that sustained me in my darkest moments. Grief is a profound and complex experience. It comes in waves—sometimes gently lapping at the edges of our hearts, and other times crashing over us like a storm we are not sure we can survive. I have walked through every phase of this storm, from the initial shock and devastation to the long, quiet days of reflection and rebuilding. I have learned that grief is not something that can be neatly contained or easily explained. It lingers, it reshapes us, and it teaches us how to live again. I often say that grief is like looking at the sun. If you look at it too long, you will go blind. If you ignore it, you will grow cold. I found that grief is a dance of looking and turning away.

This book is not just about my pain but about the amazing grace that met me in that pain. Through every tear, I felt the presence of something greater than myself—whether it was in the kindness of friends, the unexpected strength I found in prayer, or the simple, quiet moments of stillness where I felt the love of my daughters surrounding me. Grace was always there, even when I couldn't see it. Each chapter of this book holds a piece of my heart, and in sharing these stories, I hope that I have done justice to the memories of my three beautiful daughters—Imose, Chika, and Anya. They were my light, my joy, and my purpose. Losing them felt like the end of my world, but through this process, I have come to understand that their lives continue to have meaning, not just for me, but for anyone who reads these pages. Their spirits live on in the lessons they taught me: to love deeply, to be brave, and to trust in the grace that carries us through the hardest times. For those who have experienced loss, I want you to know that you are not alone. There will be days when it feels like the pain is too much to bear, but I promise you that grace will find you. It may come in the form of a sign that reminds you of a departed loved one, a helping hand, or a quiet moment of peace when you least expect it. Hold on to those moments, because they are the reminders that even in our grief, life is still worth living.

It's important to acknowledge that grief is not something we ever truly "get over." Instead, we move forward with it, and it becomes a part of who we are, a new companion we learn to live with. But in that companionship, we also find strength and resilience. The love that we carry for those we have lost never fades—it grows, transforms, and becomes part of the fabric of our lives. That fabric is much like a string in a tapestry. In the beginning you can't see the significance of that one string, but as the tapestry comes together, you see how important that single string truly was. Through That is where grace truly lives—in the love that endures, despite the pain. I could not have written this book without the unwavering support of those who have walked beside me on this journey, teaching me how to walk in strength and how to love fearlessly. To my family, my friends, and to every person who reached out to oU'er words of encouragement, thank you from the bottom of my heart. Your love and kindness gave me the strength to keep going.

And to my departed daughters—Imose, Chika, and Anya—your light continues to shine through everything I do. You have taught me what it means to live with purpose, to love without fear, and to trust in the grace that is greater than any grief. To my remaining daughters Nkiru "CeCe" and Ngozi "Zi". This book is my tribute to you, and I pray that through these words, others may find hope, healing, and strength in their own journeys. May grace find you, no matter where you are in your story.

With all my love and deepest gratitude,

Roschelle Ogbuji

ACKNOWLEDGEMENTS

First and foremost, I want to give thanks to my mother, Starling West, who was my rock throughout this entire journey. She stayed up countless nights, listening to me cry, question, and wrestle with my grief. Without her strength and unwavering support, I cannot imagine how I would have made it through. I would like to thank my father Edward West Sr. for being my first seminary teacher and teaching me that above all else faith is what keeps us going.

I would also like to thank my sister, Monique West-Fielder, and my brothers, Edward West and William Meadows, and my entire extended family for standing by me and pushing me to keep going. Your love and support have meant the world to me.

To my best friend, Brad Raymond, thank you for teaching

me that love is more than just a romantic feeling—it's a deep-seated, soul-level connection. Your friendship has been a lifeline.

My heartfelt gratitude goes to my spiritual mentors Dr. Tinu Tadese, Dottie Rieman, Minister Angela McKinney and Rev. Randy Partain. Thank you all for pushing me to deepen and widen my relationship with God and never to give up on my expectations of new experiences with the source of love. To my dear friend and author J.J. Winston, who showed me that becoming an author was a dream I could realize.

Thank you for believing in me and allowing me to follow in your footsteps.

To Tiffany Martin-Thornton, CNP of Proud to Be Me. Thank you for being my partner through this mental health journey and providing me with the tools to mental and physical wellness. The work we have done together to keep and maintain my emotional health has been life affirming.

My dear friend Andrea Walker-Stricker, words cannot express my gratitude for everything you did to get me through the initial shock of losing my children and being there for me with the birth of Ngozi and Nkiru. Thank you for believing that I had a story worth telling.

A special thanks to R.E. Woods for your incredible support and assistance throughout this writing process. Without your encouragement, this book would not exist. You walked with me through every step of reliving the trauma, pushing me to share my story because it's one that people need to hear. I am eternally grateful.

I want to thank LifeBanc and Elissa Berman, MOTEEP, and Donate Life America and the entire organ procurement community for giving me the platform to share Anya's story and the importance of organ and tissue donation. Thank you to the professionals who work tirelessly every day to encourage the gift of life.

To my faith communities, the Unitarian Universalist Congregation of Cleveland and The DePaul gospel choir, thank you for being a place where I can live my faith out loud and grow in ways I never imagined. You've provided a safe and bold space for me to heal.

To my beloved daughters, Ngozi and Nkiru, thank you for your grace as I worked through this book. You have taught me that strength can be gentle and compassionate, and that hope is something we hold onto, even in the darkest times. To Anya, Chika, and Imose, your lives continue to inspire me to live fully every day.

Thank you to the Karamu House and the many women empowerment organizations that allowed me to keep the voices of Anya, Chika, and Imose alive. Your platforms have been vital in sharing my story and honoring my daughters' legacies.

I want to thank the Shaker Heights Fire Department, the Shaker Heights Police Department, Ronald McDonald House of Cleveland, and the entire community of Northeast Ohio for surrounding me with love and prayers. Your support carried me when I didn't think I could go on.

And above all, thank you, God, for never giving up on me, for guiding me through the darkness, and for always providing light when I needed it most. I am forever grateful for the Holy Spirit's presence in my life and the strength that came through my faith in Jesus.

RESOURCES FOR HEALING

Recommended Books

A Course in Miracles – by Helen Schucman

The Bait of Satan – by John Bevere

The Body Keeps the Score – by Bessel Van Der Kolk. MD

Boundaries, Updated and Expanded Edition - by John Townsend and Henry Cloud

I Want to Trust You, but I Don't - by Lysa TerKeurst

Mindfulness Base Stress Reduction – by Jon Kabat-Zinn

Untangle Your Emotions - by Jennie Allen

When Religion Hurts You - by Laura E. Anderson PhD

Amazing Organizations

Cornerstone of Hope
www.cornerstoneofhope.org

Donate Life of America
www.donatelife.net

LifeBanc
www.lifebanc.org

MOTTEP
www.natlmottep.org